Wholeness

TREVOR ROWE

Wholeness

BODY, MIND AND SPIRIT—
ONE MAN

London EPWORTH PRESS

© Trevor Rowe 1976
First published 1976
by Epworth Press
All rights reserved

7162 0258 1

Enquiries should be addressed to
The Methodist Publishing House
Wellington Road
Wimbledon
London SW19 8EU
Printed in Great Britain by
The Garden City Press Limited
Letchworth, Hertfordshire SG6 1JS

Contents

Acknowledgements

Biblical texts are taken from the
Jerusalem Bible © 1966, 1967, 1969,
published by Darton, Longman & Todd Ltd,
and used by permission of the publisher,
and from the *New English Bible*,
2nd edition © 1970, by permission of
Oxford and Cambridge University Presses.

Introduction

Early in the Church's history Tertullian wrote the startling sentence: 'The flesh is the hinge of Salvation' (*Caro salutis est cardo*). This book is intended to encourage groups of Christians to explore together the ways in which *salvation* can come to them; not by ignoring their bodies or in some way overcoming them, but by working to restore the harmony of, to use traditional terms, body, mind and spirit. The aim is health or wholeness—enabling all the aspects of the person to interact with each other in complementary rather than competitive ways. Adapting a biblical text we can say: 'What God has joined together, man must not separate.' God has provided physical, emotional, mental and spiritual contexts within which man lives. One aspect of salvation is the bringing of what we experience in these contexts into coherence with each other.

The Christian tradition is not without ambiguity concerning this subject. It has often seemed that Christians have despised the body and seen it as an enemy to be overcome. It will repay some effort to examine the roots of the Christian tradition in the Bible and see how distortions have arisen. We need to review our attitudes, at both intellectual and emotional levels, if we are to be in a position to appreciate and use some of the techniques that have developed recently and which can help us in our quest for wholeness.

One essential for benefiting from this exploration is a readiness not only to have our attitudes reshaped by the biblical tradition but to be open to ideas that are current in many secular disciplines. If we are to achieve health we must indeed look to Christ for it, but not feel it is in any way disloyal to turn for help also to yoga, the 'human potential movement' and many other places.

The Queen's College　　　　　T R E V O R   R O W E
Birmingham

1 Biblical foundations

When you first learn to drive a car you tend to think of things separately. 'Now is the time to change gear—first push in the clutch. . . . There is a pedestrian about to cross the road—what do I do? . . .' But there comes a time when the driver and the car become one. We can respond to the car, the road conditions and ourselves quite naturally. Then driving can be a joy. We know that it is artificial to separate out different parts of what we are and look at them. What I think and what I feel are closely related, but it is useful sometimes to look at them separately as long as we do not fall for the idea that they are really distinct things. My body and my spirit belong to each other and it is artificial to think of them as two separable entities. I experience health when all that I am is functioning harmoniously and I do not need to think about the parts that go to make up the whole. If, while driving, I hear a clanking under the bonnet I begin to feel anxious and my concentration on the road relaxes. A fault in a part destroys the harmony of the whole. Similarly a sudden pain in the chest lets loose a whole set of reactions that we can analyse out as thoughts, emotions, palpitations—but it is really a single experience.

This view of man as essentially a single entity is

found in the Bible. The Genesis stories read: 'God created man in his own image' and 'God formed a man from the dust of the ground and breathed into his nostrils the breath of life' (Genesis 1:27, 2:7). What is meant by 'in his own image' has been the subject of much dispute, but at least it must mean that man is 'single' as God is. Man is a unity. The material and the spiritual were so brought together that there was made a distinct creature. Of course, the Hebrews, like us, were capable of looking at the body of man on its own. They were able to explore the variety of emotions and thoughts they experienced. But they did not set one part over against the other. They certainly did not see one part of man as better than the other. 'God saw all that he had made, and it was very good' (Genesis 1:31).

In order to wean ourselves out of a way of looking at man that depends, often unconsciously, upon seeing body and soul as separate, we shall have to absorb the Hebrew attitude by long reading of the Bible. Here we can only refer to a few biblical passages.

The word 'flesh' is used in the Old Testament in ways that indicate that it was seen as more than 'mere flesh'—that is, more than in physical terms alone. Using the characteristic of Hebrew poetry that depends on repeating the same idea in two ways, the Psalmist says:

> 'God, you are my God, I am seeking you,
>   my soul is thirsting for you,

my flesh is longing for you.'
(Psalm 63 : 1 *Jerusalem*)

Similarly 'breath' is used of the breath a man breathes
and the life that animates his body. God

'gave breath to (the earth's) people
and life to the creatures that move in it.'
(Isaiah 42 : 5)

Just as flesh and soul are two sides of the coin—man
—so are breath and life. We are not dealing with a
jigsaw puzzle. Flesh and soul, breath and life are not
separate pieces that fit together and make man. They
are ways of speaking of the one thing: man. Of
course, the Israelites were able to distinguish between
soul and body but they saw them so intimately united
that the distinction was never pressed.

In the New Testament we find a similar way of
looking at man. The *New English Bible* translates
Paul's exhortation to the Roman Christians: 'Offer
your very selves' to God. The Greek literally means
'living bodies' (12 : 1). The 'body' is the whole man.
When I say, 'I have a pain in my leg', I seem to be
suggesting that my leg is something other than me—
it is like 'my handkerchief in my pocket'. But the flesh,
or the parts of the body, in the New Testament are the
means by which the life of man is expressed. So when
slaves are told to obey their masters 'according to the
flesh' (Ephesians 6 : 5), what is implied by 'flesh' is the
historically and socially determined situation in which

11

they find themselves. However, one feature of this situation is that man sets himself over against God and this opposition is often expressed in terms of 'flesh' against 'spirit'. But it is important not to see this as suggesting that it is because of man's physical nature that he opposes God. Here 'flesh' stands for man—for that aspect of man's nature as a whole that fails to take God into account. In the *New English Bible* many of the familiar distinctions are lost in the paraphrasing style—for example, 'lower nature' replaces 'flesh'. So the contrast is made between a man being directed by his 'lower nature' and by 'the Spirit'. This does express quite well the meaning. The trouble is that many people have had their views shaped by a less subtle tradition and have assumed that, in some way, physicality is opposed to God.

The fact that this cannot be so is made clear in the Incarnation. 'The Word became flesh.' The whole message of the New Testament is, as Tertullian later saw it, that salvation comes to us through the flesh. It can come in no other way, because this is what we are: people of flesh who receive all that we are through the senses. So 'in Christ the complete being of the Godhead dwells embodied' (Collossians 2:9). Peter had to come to terms with the voice saying, 'It is not for you to call profane what God counts clean' (Acts 11:9) against a social and religious tradition that had encouraged him to see certain foods as profane and unclean. Christians have to free themselves from traditions that inhibit them from accepting the central message of Christianity as a true incarnation. It is in man that God acts for the salvation of man. So we find the New Testament writers attacking views that would tend to diminish the importance of the bodiliness of Jesus. They are 'deceivers . . . who do not acknowledge Jesus Christ as coming in the flesh' (2 John 7).

When we move outside the New Testament we see the tendency the New Testament writers hint at finding full expression. There are views of Christ which suggest that he only appeared to possess a human body—he was a particularly realistic apparition. We find those who seem to disdain the body and value only a disincarnate 'knowledge'. But chiefly Christianity became influenced by Greek ways of thinking and in particular the thought of Plato. The view became widely held that the soul, being eternal, was independent of and superior to the body. Whilst extreme views, as in Manichaeism in which the physical was repudiated, were condemned by the Church, the view that saw an inferior value in the physical gained a hold in popular religion. Some of the early Fathers gave such views support by extravagant statements, but more generally dichotomies between body and soul, matter and spirit became part of the framework within which people thought. Souls tended to be seen as more important than bodies and spiritual things of greater significance than material.

Against the pressure of this tradition we have to build our attitudes on the foundation of the

Incarnation. Jesus was not only flesh and soul, he was the one in whom 'flesh' (the historically and socially determined situation in which he found himself) did take God into account. He is the model for us of the integrated human being—at harmony within himself and with the external world as well as at one with God. Jesus is not just a demonstration. His healing ministry is the beginning of a process by which God restores health to mankind. Jesus came to the world not just announcing the Good News but putting it to work among the poor, the prisoners, the blind, the broken. To some he gave the physical change that brought them health; to others he gave forgiveness and made them free. What was both declared and begun in Christ has been continuing ever since. Sometimes the Good News has been distorted and become a source of illness in human life, but constantly the Church has been attempting to see the Gospel clearly and completely so that it becomes in the first place an illuminator of what is dark in man's life and secondly the power to bring healing.

It is this evangelical aim that we are here seeking to pursue.

Books

A. R. Johnson, *The Vitality of the Individual in the Thought of Ancient Israel* (Wales University Press, 1964).

C. A. Van Peursen, *Body, Soul, Spirit: A Survey of*

the Body-Mind Problem (Oxford University Press, 1966).

W. Strawson in *Mental Health and the Church* (The Methodist Church Division of Social Responsibility, 1975).

Group work

1. Let the group make a list of various familiar activities concerned with different aspects of human life, e.g. eating an ice cream cornet; reading a book; laughing at a joke. . . . Then let each person put the activities in order of importance, as he or she sees it. Discuss together why you rank some things as more important than others. Particularly note the difference in importance given by different people.

2. Look up some biblical passages and see if they mean the same to all members of the group e.g. Isaiah 40:6–8, 12f., Psalm 63, Job 10:1 f., Romans 12:1 f., Romans 8:5 f.

3. 'The unassumed is the unhealed.' This statement was used in the early Church to make the point that unless Christ assumed human nature he could not heal it. Is this how you see it?

2 Facets of the person

When C. G. Jung attempted to classify people according to the dominant features of their personalities, he wrote of four functions which we use to orientate ourselves in the world. These were: thinking, feeling, sensation and intuition. These activities we can see taking place within four sub-worlds that together make up the one world in which a man lives. Man has a thinking life in which the images in his mind are organized into useful concepts. He also has a life within a world of feeling. Most of the stimuli come to man through the senses. It is this capacity to sense the external world that we recognize as absent in a person so damaged that we call him 'vegetable'. But Jung was right to draw attention to a sub-world in man that is distinguishable from thought, feeling and sensation. Intuition operates to transmit perceptions in an unconscious way. When I think, reason links up the ideas. When I feel or sense, I can relate my feeling or sensation to some recognizable stimulus. But within man's experience is this fourth world—a world inhabited by ideas, the source of which is hidden. Jung was right to perceive that what we know intuitively has 'an intrinsic character of certainty and conviction'. We know the things we sense are real. A similar level of conviction applies to our intuitions.

Always remembering that these four sub-worlds are part of the one world of a man's life we can look at them a little more closely—to see their importance for us and the ways in which they relate to each other.

It is the mind of man that has enabled him to explore the world so fully. Modern scientific enterprise rests firmly on the capacity of the mind to think mathematically—that is, to produce a way of organizing dimensions and relationships within the physical world that can serve as a tool for predicting what will happen when we manipulate physical objects. We have a way of causing to happen what we choose to happen. But prior to control is understanding and when our understanding takes a shape that satisfies a need for harmony, which appears to be a goal all human endeavour is engaged in seeking, we can say we have discovered meaning. There are great delights to be experienced in this intellectual world. As Julian Huxley once remarked: 'It is nice to know things'. It may be hard for those who have been encouraged or allowed to find mathematics difficult to believe that there is great joy in working out a mathematical problem—but it is so. The world is fascinating. The problems in understanding it are absorbing. The ways in which men have sought to find meaning in life can stimulate an unending curiosity. Yet thinking can be a way of defending ourselves from other experiences that we may not find so easy to control.

We can shut ourselves up in an intellectual world. We recognize the existence of our bodies, emotions and the world around us, but we prefer to keep them at a distance from our minds. It is in the world of thought that we really live. This so-called schizoid orientation is not uncommon. A man can have an image of fatherhood in his mind and it is this image of what he thinks a father ought to be that determines his behaviour as far as his children are concerned. But the children want to relate to a person who is a father, and they only meet an abstraction. Most people have abstract images and ideals that motivate them. The personal is sacrificed to the image and we feel we are in contact with an idea not a person. Though this is not a happy stance to adopt it is chosen as the better of two evils. If I can justify myself to myself in terms of my image then I do not need to care about what others think of me. Of course I do care—care deeply —and so I must defend myself against possible rejection by others by retreating into this safe mental world that I can more or less control. Thus I am crippled.

Man lives a sterile life if it lacks full emotional experience (I am giving an emotional emphasis to Jung's concept of feeling). We need to experience warmth, tenderness, love on the one hand, and rejection, aggression, hate on the other. These feelings are a natural part of living in contact with other human beings. We are not going to be liked by everyone and our opinions are not going to win universal support. So we feel rejection—that is the normal price of honest relationships. People will frustrate my expectations and I shall feel aggression arising out of my frustration. Love is the feeling that comes when I choose to give value to another person. I can choose the opposite, and in devaluing another feel hate. So warmth and tenderness can come as we or others make the opposite choices from those that result in rejection and aggression. Without emotional colour to life it seems insipid; but allowing oneself to feel in a full sense is dangerous. If I engage in argument at a purely intellectual level I am happy to follow the logic where it leads, but the moment I let emotion in the possibility of pain arises. If you feel love for someone your potential for being hurt by them is very great. We have all known people who have been deeply hurt and who resist entering any other intimate relationship for fear of burning their fingers again. Most people have learnt this in less extreme forms and keep a distance between themselves and others and thus set limits to their capacity to feel.

The link between sensory and emotional experience is very close. The way in which we tend to describe behaviour and feelings in bodily terms shows this. We talk of shouldering burdens, being heartbroken, having butterflies in the stomach, and so on. The link is recognized in common speech. It is also widely recognized that emotional states can affect bodily states. When a person's emotions cannot be adequately discharged they can be redirected toward the body and their attack shows itself in gastric ulcers or a coronary thrombosis. Because this link is so close and we are vulnerable to too much feeling, it seems we deaden our senses so that we can live within a restricted world that we find manageable. If I walk along with my head in the clouds I do not see the old lady trying to cross the road through heavy traffic and so feel no conscience in neglecting her. We choose unconsciously, and yet deliberately, to narrow our sensory awareness to what we can take. If I develop skill in interpreting the non-verbal signals that come to me in facial expressions and other bodily movements, then my emotional sympathies may be aroused by the people around me, sometimes to an intolerable extent. Therefore the tendency is to desensitize the senses so that life keeps within chosen limits—dull but tolerable.

Not only is the sensate world that which impinges on our bodies externally. We sense also what is going on within our bodies. The trouble is that our awareness of our own bodies often moves in a hypochondriacal way. We feel pain or discomfort and see it as a threat—an intrusion—so we turn to the medical expert to get rid of this for us and from us. We are not so sensitive to the normal feeling of our bodies. We cannot so easily feel tension in muscles and locate the points where our anxiety is impinging within our body. Conversely neither are we able, because of this way in which we restrict the flow of sensuous experience, to know to its fullest extent the joy of bodily experience.

Of all the sub-worlds within man's experience none

is more vital than what we have called intuition. None is more undervalued. The difficulty is that though we are most sure of our intuitions we cannot support them by recognizable methods of verification. The mind is ruled by rationality and if there is a logical coherence to my ideas I can believe in their truth. Emotions can be justified by the common experience of man. If I am treated unjustly I feel resentment. If I describe this experience to others they recognize it —it coheres with general human experience. Sense experience is related to the reality of the physical world. My experience of it coheres with the descriptions others make and we call the common object of our descriptions physical reality. But I can bring forward no support for my intuitions. This is a world in which faith operates—but not only faith. Salvation—wholeness—healing—comes to us when we open ourselves to what comes in this intuitive or faith world. A series of Reformed theologians, from Luther, through Barth and Bonhoeffer, to Bultmann, have been attempting to show us that when we can support the stance we take to life in some way, we have not got Christian faith. You cannot save yourself by works, knowledge, religious practices and historical certainty. Only an unsupported faith, as it were, clears the lines of communication between our sub-worlds and enables them to function harmoniously.

We shall be aiming in the following chapters to explore ways in which these lines of communication can be re-opened.

Books

C. G. Jung, *Modern Man in Search of a Soul* (Routledge and Kegan Paul, 1961).

C. G. Jung, *Psychological Types* (Routledge and Kegan Paul, 1923).

A. Lowen, *The Betrayal of the Body* (Collier Books, New York, 1976).

Group work

1. Play 'I am a Rock' from Simon and Garfunkel's record *The Sound of Silence* and discuss the lines:

> 'Safe within my womb
> I touch no one and no one touches me.
> I am a Rock, I am an Island.
> And a rock feels no pain;
> And an island never cries.'

2. Share together ways in which you keep people at a distance.

3. How do you feel about 'being angry' or 'crying'?

4. Can you put into words some deep conviction that you find it difficult to justify?

3 Learning to relax

A teacher of Yoga assures me that the vast majority of those who attend her classes come with one primary aim: to learn to relax. The evidence is all around us that people live not just under tension but with tension—that is, it is not only true that the modern world exerts pressures upon us, but we do not know how to dissipate the tension that results. The Christian spiritual tradition has made many discoveries about how men can find a quality of peace, not achieved by avoiding conflict, but through contact with normal life. Somehow the Church has failed to make this available and alternatives are being sought elsewhere.

As we have seen the body and mind interact closely with each other. If peace of mind is to be achieved this will be assisted by a relaxed body. Similarly we can teach our bodies to relax through our minds. So we must approach coping with tension along two lines—neither of which is superior to the other. They are complementary.

Firstly, there are methods for cultivating a quiet mind. At this point we shall mention only very simple things. We can restore to ourselves the gift of silence. It may require considerable effort to find it. Noise is endemic in our world and environmentalists are

right to draw attention to the erosion of our quality
of life caused by increased noise in our surroundings.
Many people need noise like a drug. It seems to be
necessary to fill a gap. Silence appears as a threat.
Yet those who have faced this threat and worked
through it have found the search for silence to be a
road to peace. At first there may be 'withdrawal
symptoms' not altogether dissimilar to those experienced when an addictive drug is withdrawn, as when
one gives up smoking. Silence is not immediately
welcomed. The emptiness is oppressive. Gradually
silence eats its way into our hearts and a peace
develops in which important transactions can take
place within us and between ourselves and God.
Many people are seeking these experiences in the
traditional silent retreat. Silence, though, is not the
only way of quietening the frenetic nature of life.
One can take away any of the things we have become
used to and find that once the customary rhythm of
the world is broken there comes an opportunity to
discover alternative and more peaceful patterns. I
have found it helpful deliberately to disengage from
the intellectual world that occupies a large part of
my attention during the week. The method I chose
was to spend Saturday mornings doing sculpture. A
quite different set of faculties was brought into play
and the mind could take a rest. 'Retreats' need not
only be on a classic silent pattern. A retreat could
be any type of activity in which a familiar stabilising

feature of life is taken away and thus a new pattern allowed to emerge.

One of the more imaginative ventures of a suburban church I know is to open their church one evening to anyone who would like to come to enjoy quiet. A programme of recorded music is played. Silence is not offered, but quiet is. This is the 'world writing the agenda'—a church responding to the needs of commuters thirsting for quietness. I was visiting a house where the wife was very ill. I too was under tension at the time and this was recognized by the husband. Before I left he invited me into his 'den' sat me down and played for me what he knew to be a favourite piece of music. After a while I left, hoping that I could be as good a pastor as my friend had been to me.

Not to be forgotten is the importance of adequate time for sleep and how we cope with the problem of being unable to sleep. We shall not be able to relax if we deny ourselves the most natural form of relaxation: sleep. Learning to relax when sleep does not come is hard for those for whom insomnia is rare. I can offer little at this point except the technique of 'paradoxical intention'. It is suggested that sometimes we fail to sleep because we are too intent on doing so. Instead of trying to sleep try to do the opposite, that is, to stay awake as long as possible. When we, as it were, de-fuse our anxiety about sleeplessness we fall asleep quite naturally. I have little experience to suggest how frequently this technique works.

Then there are methods that start with the body and seek to bring relaxation to the whole person, beginning by taking tension from the muscles. Two methods are moderately easy to use. The first, relaxation, you can do for yourself. The second, massage, requires a partner.

Relaxation of the body is quite simple. What you do is systematically to put the muscles under tension and then allow them to relax. Lie down on the floor. If you are going to maintain the relaxation for some time it may be well to cover yourself with a blanket. It is also useful to reduce the lighting. Lie flat on your back with your arms by your sides and feet a few inches apart. Then work through your body. First tighten the muscles of your feet and then release the tension. Tighten the ankles and let go. Then the calves. Press the knees towards the floor and relax. Tighten the thigh and let go; the buttocks; the lower abdomen. Curve the spine away from the floor and then relax. Take a deep breath and as you breath out let the whole chest relax. Tighten the neck muscles—pull your head off the floor—and let go. Screw up the facial muscles—it does not matter what you look like—and relax. Tighten the shoulders and let go. Work down the arms—tighten and relax, until the whole body from toes to the tips of your fingers is relaxed. Let yourself feel as though you were falling through the floor—or spreading out over it. Now let your mind float along with your body. Sometimes it will be possible to see yourself drifting, as in flight,

26

over familiar places—those places perhaps that linger in the memory from holidays. Fly away where you will. Spelling it out in words like this sounds very silly. In fact it is a marvellous experience.

The ability to relax the body also enhances other functions. Speech trainers these days teach relaxation because they know that if the body is not relaxed the voice will be restricted. Certainly the width and depth of emotion conveyed in the voice will be constrained. Just as the emotions affect the body so tensions within the body limit the extent of the emotional response of which the person is capable. Some people cannot enjoy a belly-laugh because their bellies will not let them. The abdominal muscles are so tight that the emotion, as it were, has no room to grow. Not only does the sort of tension of which we have been speaking destroy peace in the negative sense, it also prevents positive developments in the person taking place.

Currently massage has a bad name. It will be a pity if the abuse of massage means that its benefits are not explored. A brief account here will not be adequate and those who want to explore the skill more fully will find a number of manuals readily available. Some of these have somewhat sensational titles and use illustrations and covers that the prudish may find embarrassing. Such embarrassment may be a signal that you would greatly benefit from the experience.

Beside the relaxation massage can give there is the

27

additional benefit of simply being touched in a careful way by another person. At this point we shall regard this inter-personal contact as just a delightful added bonus. Here our chief concern is with tense muscles.

As with most skills, the power one has to relax muscles through massage can be improved with training. But it is a very ordinary skill and no mystique needs to be attached to it. It is a skill learnt by doing—all you need are your hands and a gentleness of attitude towards the other person. The illustrations in books will show the massaging of a naked body. This may be what a couple choose, but it is not absolutely necessary. The floor will serve as a massaging table. To know something of the muscular system may help, but sensitive fingers will discover the muscles in no time. Begin by trying to get your partner into a relaxed mood. You may like to talk gently to create a tender mood. Or you may begin with gentle strokes on the face, neck or hand. As together you feel you are relaxing, your hands and fingers can discover the contours of the other's body and massage proper begins.

Four easy-to-perform types of massage strokes can be mentioned. 1. There are long steady strokes delivered with the flat of the hand, the fingers, or thumb towards the centre of the body. 2. A gentle rolling or squeezing of the tissues that have been lifted away from the bony substructures. 3. The slapping that we have seen vigorously administered in films can become a much more gentle stroke—the sides of the hands or the fingertips rapidly jostling the flesh. 4. Circular movements with the palm, fingers, thumb or knuckles. With these possible movements in the back of the mind a person with care in his heart can help the person he cares for to relax. The person receiving the massage can guide the partner to the muscles where tension is felt. It is a shared experience.

All I would recommend is gentle exploration of massage as a relaxing procedure. This exploration may lead naturally into a more developed procedure and here people would be advised to look for a manual that treats the subject in detail. But it should be said clearly that people with high blood pressure, heart trouble or diabetes should not receive amateur massage. More obviously it would be foolish to engage in massage where there are torn ligaments, broken limbs, skin abrasions and the like. Insensitive massage—too much pressure on soft tissues—would be painful and foolish. Massage should only continue as long as it is desired. The purpose of the exercise is to relax, not exhaust.

The methods of relaxation we have mentioned here vary considerably and what may be suitable for one will be unhelpful to the other. The paradox is that one has to work at relaxing—but not too much.

Books
J. M. Wallace, *Relaxation—a key to better living* (Max Parrish, 1965).

Byron Scott, *How the Body Feels* (Ballantine Books, New York, 1973).

George Downing, *The Massage Book* (Penguin, 1975).

Group work

1. 'That the birds of worry and care fly above your head, this you cannot change, but that they build nests in your hair, this you can prevent.' Can you?

2. Be silent together for a period and then discuss the experience.

3. Share your different methods of relaxing.

4. Do the relaxation exercise together—one of you talking the rest through the tighten-relax routine.

5. If you care to, try some gentle massage, e.g. massage another person's hands, or shoulder muscles, or foot.

4 Repossessing the body

A. H. Maslow constructed a theory of motivation from the idea that people do things to meet their needs and that these needs are arranged in a hierarchy —the appearance of one need rests on the prior satisfaction of another more pressing need. So we have basic physiological needs and unless these are met we are not interested in anything else. A baby cries when its survival is threatened: when it is hungry, or cold, or hurt. Physiological needs are primary. But if these are satisfied safety needs appear. So a child needs a predictably organized world: something to count on. When our world is safe then we are free to desire association with others, and beyond that there is need for esteem and finally, what Maslow called, 'self-actualization'. It is not surprising that Maslow before his death was closely involved in movements in North America that attempted to help people realize their full potential as human beings. This concern for self-actualization or achieving full human potential, which is also the concern of this book, is something of a luxury. We are not likely to be interested in it unless more basic needs have been met. Most of these in Western society are routinely satisfied. Physiological and safety needs are adequately met. We have organized our world so that this is so—at least for us. We have everything from supermarkets to insurance policies to take care of these needs. Love or association cannot be so easily organized, but we have our ways. We do not just depend upon people seeking each other out, we create social pressures to move people into association and provide institutions, from clubs to pubs, as frameworks within which it can happen. It is not surprising that developed societies create 'meritocracy': when we have climbed so far up the hierarchy of needs we look for ways of establishing esteem. Vance Packard could write about 'The Status Seekers' in a well-fed, safe, society in which the nuclear family provided satisfaction and its defects could be balanced by drawing on the resources of various supplementary social organizations. Most people in the world do not climb as far as this in the hierarchy of needs—never mind self-actualization. So if we are to explore this further it must be with a sense of privilege.

The human potential movement has taken a number of lines. All are concerned in one way or another with the integration of the body, emotions, mind and spirit. Some put greater emphasis than others on different aspects of this integration, but it would receive general assent from them all that the goal they were seeking was wholeness understood in some way or other. We cannot hope to describe all these lines, but we shall seek to indicate features of some of them.

We need to give more attention to our bodies. This is not simply an appeal to keep physically fit— although it is included. We know that a number of serious illnesses can be prevented by regular and vigorous exercise. But here we are concerned not simply with an athletic body, but one that functions smoothly and effectively. This means giving the body attention or becoming more aware of the body. Again this needs to be qualified. We are not commending either pampering the body or becoming so concerned about our bodies that we become hypochondriacs. Rather the aim is to be able to experience bodily functions more completely in such a way that we can use our bodies to enjoy life more fully.

When we were describing relaxation we indicated that one can deliberately first tense muscles in order to allow them to relax. In this way we become aware of parts of our bodies and can feel where tension is focused. Certain exercises can help to show the way in which some forms of anxiety express themselves in areas of the body. Close your eyes and imagine that you want to be somewhere else but are being prevented from getting there. In this fantasy anxiety will be raised and you will feel it in some part of the body. Some people will feel a tightening of the chest; others will feel it in their legs as though they are digging in their heels in a tug-of-war; others in their fists as though they want to do battle with the one who is restraining them.

33

We are conditioned by social training to control the physical responses that are natural in certain circumstances. When we are abused in some way it is natural to hit out at the assailant. Children show this naturalness, but we put constraints upon it. These constraints are necessary, as uncontrolled responses would lead to unacceptable violence in social relations. But there is a difference between control and what we have learnt to call repression. When, say, a parent reprimands us for making a natural physical response to a situation we can draw the conclusion that the response is unacceptable to the one whose love we value so highly. For fear of losing love we come to regard the physical response as bad and so what we sense to be unacceptable to others becomes unacceptable to us—we split it off as not us and exile it from our conscious life. Thus when we face frustration our natural responses are blocked. Aggression is not bad in itself. It can be used destructively but also creatively, and we are not free to choose one or the other unless we can learn afresh to feel aggression and express it in physical form. If, say, we lie on the floor and pound our feet and fists we can sometimes release angry feelings that have been pent up inside us. Alternatively we can burn up our aggression openly by pounding a cushion. These are somewhat stylized exercises that can do what is often achieved with complete social acceptance on the football field, the squash court or the golf course.

Another area in which our bodily awareness can be

expanded is in our relations with others. Every society creates norms about what physical contact is acceptable between people. In Western society, outside the family, casual bodily contact is restricted to the hands. We can touch people but only in stylized ways, as for example, shaking hands. But these contacts are restricted to certain circumstances and we have to learn when we may and may not shake hands. So the Englishman goes to France and finds himself embarrassed by the frequency of hand shaking required in French culture. When we keep within the social norms for touching all is well. If we deviate from them we feel anxious ourselves and sense that our conduct raises anxiety in others. So if on meeting a stranger I were to throw my arms round him the chances are he would be nonplussed, not knowing quite how to react to an abnormal situation. People are travelling more widely these days and are coming into contact with cultures where greater bodily contact is acceptable and we are discovering that it is enjoyable once we have got beyond our culturally in-built reaction against it. An example of this cultural difference is the fact that, except in sport, in this country the amount of contact acceptable between adult males is very restricted; females are allowed more. But in both Asia and Africa males may hold hands without any suggestion of abnormality.

The heart of our problem may be that the only connotation we consider for bodily contact is sexual.

If a man touches a woman it is for sexual purposes. If a man touches a man homosexuality is suspected. From time to time we may have experiences that indicate that this is not always so. As a pastor I have held the hands of many men and women. It is simply a human act of care to provide, as it were, a shoulder to cry on. In a crisis we are prepared to offer bodily contact beyond the social norms. How silly to allow these experiences to be embarrassing rather than joyful memories. The mother who 'kisses it better' is close to human needs that do not disappear as we become more sophisticated. Children can be starved of food, love and bodily contact. So can adults and if we were prepared to believe that it is not only sexuality that can be conveyed through bodily contact we might recover a new dimension of joy in living.

Books
W. C. Schutz, *Joy—Expanding Human Awareness* (Pelican, 1973).
Michael Argyle, *The Psychology of Interpersonal Behaviour* (Pelican, 1972).
Carl R. Rogers, *Encounter Groups* (Pelican, 1973).

Group work
1. How embarrassed does it make you to talk about your body? Discuss this together.

2. Do the fantasy exercise to try to locate the points where anxiety impinges in the body. Share what you find.

3. Experiment with the aggression expressing exercise. Discuss your feelings afterwards.

4. How much do you touch different people—close relatives, friends, strangers? Can you think of crises when human touch was very important?

5 Repossessing the emotions

In the last chapter we were concerned with extending our awareness of our bodies. In this chapter we shall be concerned with repossessing our emotions or finding ways that help us to feel more fully.

Popular songs do not appear with lyrics telling us of two lovers walking to the post-box together and finding it a very matter-of-fact experience. They tend to speak of the ecstacies or sufferings of love. Important emotions have the power to gladden or hurt and it is not always possible to control which it is going to be. We have all had experiences in which we have prepared an occasion—an evening out, an excursion, a holiday. It is going to be perfect, but the loved person does not want it to be the way we want it to be and our fantasy is spoiled and we feel desolate. Because we live in a personal world where the reactions of others to us are very important, both pain and joy are always round the corner and we are never sure which we shall meet. Maybe there are brave people who are prepared to take what comes, be it pain or joy. Most of us do not like pain and we find ways of avoiding it. Two obvious ways are open. We can limit the opportunities for pain by reducing the contacts we have with potential sources of pain: people. If I keep myself to myself I may be lonely—

and that will hurt—but I do not run the risk of the big hurts other people may inflict on me. The other tack is to build up resistance against feeling too much. We become thick-skinned or hard. My experience is that people make great mistakes in estimating the thickness of skin or hardness of both themselves and other people. 'I don't care what other people say' often seems to mean the opposite. Nevertheless, the threshold for feeling appears to go up as we age. When we are young we feel intensely and show it. In adolescence similarly we feel deeply but hide our feelings. Adulthood tends to be a time when we opt out of feeling to a large extent. Surely this is a wrong move. The adult can and should recover feeling and make use of it.

The *Encounter Group* has swept through certain segments of American and British life as a context in which people have learnt to repossess their emotions. Sometimes this has come through attention to the body. They have experienced the feeling of aggression to an extent they had previously not allowed to themselves by beating a pillow with their fists. Or they have allowed themselves to feel affection as they have touched others. The trouble with so many things is that they are spoilt by enthusiasts. Stories circulate about encounter groups in which people take off their clothes or violent anger is encouraged. Why is it that people think they can only be serious about something if they take it to extremes? I am deeply convinced about the value that would come to British culture if there were greater emotional openness and more bodily contact between people. But I believe these values will only be made available generally if the change is moderate. There is a selfishness about enthusiasts for they find great value for themselves in their experiences, but alienate the majority who cannot cope with extremes. So the few gain much and the many lose. Many people would find considerable enrichment if the mystique of the encounter group could be taken away and ordinary people in an ordinary way took adventures together in opening up deeper contacts between each other. In the process they would find themselves developing a much greater width and depth of emotional experience.

Here are some exercises that have been used by many people with profit. Trust is an important emotion. We may make mistakes in judgement concerning other people and find that they are not as trustworthy as we imagined. So the experience of failure encourages us to restrict our feeling of trust. We protect ourselves for fear of failure in discriminating correctly between who is trustworthy and who is not. *Log-rolling* is an exercise often used to repossess a feeling of trust. A group of people stand closely together in a circle facing inwards. One person stands in the centre, closes his eyes and allows himself to fall outwards while keeping his feet in the same place with legs and arms straight. A person in the outer group catches him and pushes him towards another member of the group. It looks as though the person in the centre is a log being pushed about, but the experience is very different. The group experience the man or woman in the centre very much as a person for whom they are responsible and the person in the centre begins to recognize the trustworthiness of the group. He knows that they will not let him fall and begins to feel trust as an emotion developing within him. I remember a woman who was a member of a group that played the exercise together. As a girl she had spent many months in plaster after receiving a back injury when someone pulled a chair away as she was about to sit in it. Understandably enough she had never found it easy to trust people physically but she played the game and found herself experiencing trust in a way she had not allowed herself since the accident.

Many emotions are smothered because we are not prepared to believe that they are generally experienced in the circumstances that prompt them in us. To discover that others feel as we do can help free us from treating perfectly straightforward feelings as guilty secrets. The following exercise can only be done with an element of surprise. The leader tells the group that in a short while he wants one of them to volunteer to do something—perhaps it could be to tell the others something they have never told anyone else before. After a pause, he then says that he does not in fact want such a volunteer but wants them to focus on their feelings when he gave them notice of his impending request. The group can share their feelings of fear and anxiety—the conflict between wanting to co-operate with the leader and not wanting to let out a secret—and so on. The sharing that follows this sort of exercise reveals that people tend to feel in similar ways if they are prepared to recognize their feelings. One very important problem in life generally is not just that people will not face conflict honestly, but they cannot always find ways of expressing agreement. For example, members of a family all put up with something because they believe that the other members like it. They cannot find a way of agreeing. (This has been called the *Abilene Paradox* by J. B. Harvey and applied to some problems of industry and government.) We can be encouraged to feel more fully when we find ways for recognizing that our feelings are shared—that the emotion promoted in us by a situation is a common one.

It is easy to get into the habit of thinking negatively rather than positively about people. It is also easy to suppose that other people do this too and that we are therefore the objects of critical rather than affirmatory opinions. We can deliberately reverse this process. We know very well what it feels like to be criticised and we allow this feeling to maintain itself within us when there is no justification for it. We can repossess the feeling of being appreciated by the exercise of *strength bombardment*. Members of a group in turn go round the other members of the group saying in a sentence or two what they regard as the strengths or qualities they admire in the other person. Criticism is banished and deliberately replaced by affirmation. It is a strange experience to be seated some distance round the circle and experiencing a sense of doom because one cannot believe that the person making the rounds will have found anything good to say about oneself, and then there is something, and when we hear it it feels like receiving a most generous gift. The feeling of gratitude once released may then find other ways of being experienced.

Sometimes there is a side to our personality that is somewhat muted. We know it is there but we are a little unsure of ourselves concerning it. We feel that if we brought it out more fully it would appear incongruous alongside the image of ourselves with which other people are familiar. Very often groups of people have a capacity for recognizing an unfulfilled part of another's character. One exercise that encourages this is for the group to give new names to the members. A name will be suggested and not feel right to the group, but finally a name will emerge that fits. Let the person wear this name, as it were—get used to it and explore its implications. In all probability it will express some less obvious part of the personality. The fact that it is recognized, even though somewhat obliquely, is likely to give the person a feeling of greater confidence in exercising this undeveloped part of themselves.

Trust, gratitude, confidence—these are but a few

of the emotions that tend to be muted in our normal experience. They and many others can enrich our lives if the threshold of our experience of them is lowered and we repossess them. Of course, we take risks of being hurt as emotions are allowed a more important place in our lives. But we may find out that the balance-of-payments comes out well in our favour.

Books
as for chapter 4

Group work
1. 'Bedar, the Watchman, caught the Mulla prising open the window of his own bedroom from the outside, in the depths of night.

"What are you doing, Nasrudin? Locked out?"

"Hush! They say I walk in my sleep. I am trying to surprise myself and find out." ' (Idries Shah, *The Exploits of the Incomparable Mulla Nasrudin* (Pan Books, 1973).)

How far does your left hand know what your right hand is doing?

2. You may like to return to Simon and Garfunkel's 'I am a Rock' and see if there is more to be discovered. How thick-skinned are you? Do other people agree with your estimate?

3. Try the log-rolling exercise. Discuss your feelings together.

44

4. One member may suggest to others things they should do. Then share what it felt like to receive these suggestions.

5. Do some rounds of strength-bombardment.

6. Try the alternative name exercise.

6 Taking responsibility

One sickness in our society is that we will only trust the experts to give us health. We turn to doctors when we could very easily look after ourselves. We build into god-like figures professionals of all sorts and hand over to them responsibility for our health. How can we be healthy when we allow a sick dependency of this sort to grow? Though the experts have great skills that they can usefully make available to us in certain circumstances, the non-experts have quite adequate skills for living healthily most of the time.

On the physical side it is clear that we hand over responsibility to doctors too readily. Many illnesses do not require the attention of a doctor, only sensible action on our own part. I know how to treat a heavy cold or a normal attack of influenza just as well as a doctor. There are many things I do not know and I regard it better to save his time so that he can make available his special knowledge when I do need it. One of the valuable aspects of Dr Spock's famous book on baby care was that it helped to educate parents to take responsibility for their own children and gave indications of the points where expert help was needed. Unless we similarly take much greater responsibility for our own health than is generally the case we are likely to be overwhelmed by sickness and find the Health (or Sickness) Service in a state of complete collapse.

Similarly the psychiatrist, though not with quite the same degree of confidence, has become the expert to whom one takes mental disorder. Like physicians, the psychiatrists have available skills that are most powerful in serious cases. Many serious psychotic conditions are susceptible to treatment and this must be applied by skilled persons. The area where psychiatrists find themselves less effective is in the minor mental disorders. In this field the non-expert can, under certain conditions, be as effective as the expert. A number of developments in therapy put much more emphasis than was once the case on the role of the ordinary person sharing in his own healing and that of the ordinary person contributing to the healing of another. The crisis intervention we see at work in the Samaritans is one example of this. There are many others.

Among these developments one of the most interesting is called Gestalt Therapy. The ideal for a person is that he should function in a harmonious way. If a person's blood pressure is too high this throws other physical functions out of balance. The aim of therapy in this case is to reduce the blood pressure and restore the physical system to normal functioning. Most of the time we are keeping our bodily functions in balance by ourselves. If we are hungry we eat. If we are too cold we put on extra clothes or have a hot drink. Similarly the human being has other non-physical needs that must be met if he is to feel right. When we are able to satisfy these needs we feel happy and content. What we do is respond to our various needs to create a balance, a harmony, or to use the German word for whole: a 'Gestalt'. Sometimes we fail to a serious extent. Some aspect of our psyche behaves abnormally and throws us off balance to a marked degree. Such a situation requires the skill of a psychiatrist to get us working harmoniously again. But many times we are upset by minor disturbances and can make the readjustments ourselves and all is well. As with our bodies, so with our minds we are doing this every day. Between the very minor and the serious disturbances there is an area of 'under-par' functioning where the non-expert can also be of help. We, or preferably we-with-others, and if possible others who have taken pains to understand a bit more about how people function than that derived simply from common sense, can take responsibility for achieving our own gestalt or wholeness.

We make mistakes in responding appropriately to our various needs. I lose my temper and feel badly about it afterwards. In one way or another we come to terms with incidents like that. But there are repeated disturbing experiences that suggest there is some blockage in our system that needs to be corrected. Gestalt therapy is concerned with detecting and working upon the blockages that prevent the formation of harmony. It is suggested that these blockages arise from 1. poor perception of the external world and of our own bodies, 2. failure to express our needs openly, 3. setting limits, by muscular tightness, to what impulses we are prepared to express. People—most usefully in groups—can be helped to clear these blockages. We must look at a few of the methods that have been used to help them.

In a group wanting to help each other on gestalt therapy lines, certain rules of working will be observed. The group will always be concerned with present experience—the 'now'. The present is the most powerful experience we have and yet we tend to retreat from it. What I felt like yesterday, what I think about such-and-such; these take me away from the present. Past events do impinge on us now and these events can be brought into the present by fantasy—re-enacting the event in present terms. The group will be concerned to speak directly to each other. So often we speak as though we are aiming our words at a blank wall. 'What I dislike about some people . . .' is often an indirect way of saying 'What I dislike about you, John, is . . .'. Cut out the indirect and take the courage to speak personally. Or we say, 'A lot of people are saying . . .' when what we mean is, 'I want to say . . .', but we cannot take responsibility for our opinion. People in the group will be taking responsibility for all that is happening within them. We tend to speak of parts of our bodies or our actions as though they were third persons. So we say 'My hand is up in the air' rather than 'I am

49

holding my hand in the air'. The difference may seem trivial, but it reflects an attitude that can distort our experience. Similarly we often say, 'I can't do that', when we mean 'I won't do that'. If in the group people can be helped, by changing their language, to take responsibility, many things will be affected. If we can take pains to detect these tiny indications that we are living at a distance from our experience we shall be moving towards wholeness.

We have already looked at enhancing our awareness of the external world and of our own bodies. In gestalt therapy there is an emphasis on taking seriously some of the apparently casual things we do. When we explore these thing more fully they can be seen to be non-verbal communications—communications we dare not make openly. If we can tease out the meaning of what we are saying in a disguised way by, say, tapping our fingers or clenching our fists or looking out of the window, then our experience is enlarged. So while another person is talking I may be tapping my finger. What I want to do is beat my fist on the table and say, 'I think that is nonsense', but I have set up restraints upon the extent I permit my muscles to respond in situations like that. So no direct communication takes place. A muted communication does. If I am encouraged to exaggerate the tapping of my finger I shall probably find my true feelings coming to the surface as the restraints are loosened and so more honest, and probably less violent, communication can occur. There is a dictum of F. S. Perls, the seminal person in gestalt therapy, 'lose your mind and come to your senses'. In other words find a way into what is going on within you not through the mind, but through the senses. Concentrate not on what you are thinking but what you are doing.

After a difficult meeting we often go away saying to ourselves, 'I wish that I had said such-and-such to so-and-so'. These imaginary dialogues take place inside ourselves. One method of gestalt therapy is to bring these dialogues into the open. Sometimes an empty chair is used as a prop. In fantasy, put so-and-so in the chair and tell him what you wanted to tell him. But do not leave it there. Now take on the role of so-and-so. You sit in the chair and let him reply. So you act out the dialogue. These fantasy dialogues can be worked out between different parts of one's own personality—for example, the cautious side and the adventurous side, the flamboyant and the shy. In this way we may, literally, let the left hand know what the right hand is doing. The value of doing exercises of this sort in a group is that sympathetic friends can gently encourage us to maintain the conversation until it is complete. The temptation is to break off when honesty is becoming painful.

The exploration of dream experiences is an important aspect of gestalt therapy. Perls believed that we are the makers of our dreams. What appears in our dreams has not come from outside; we have put it there. Our dreams are coded statements to ourselves.

51

We live out in a disguised form in our dreams some of the situations we find it most difficult to handle. The technique is to re-identify all the persons and features of the dream by rehearsing the dream again and ourselves playing the parts—becoming the people and—silly as it sounds—the furniture—until we take back into ourselves what we have pushed away from ourselves in the dream image. In this process we find the dream speaking to us and interpreting ourselves to ourselves. Whereas Freud spoke of the dream as 'the royal road to the unconscious', Perls calls it 'the royal road to integration'.

The dream is but one way in which we split off parts of our experience. By honesty and taking responsibility for ourselves we can begin to draw together what we are into a whole—to begin to feel at one with ourselves.

Books
Ed. J. Fagan and I. L. Shepherd, *Gestalt Therapy Now* (Penguin, 1972).
F. Perls, R. F. Hefferline, P. Goodman, *Gestalt Therapy* (Pelican, 1973).

Group work
1. Discuss attitudes to health of members of the group. Do we rely too much on experts?
2. Apply the gestalt rules of working to the discussions of the group from now on.

3. Watch for the gestures by which restrained communications are made. Follow them through to find out what is being said.

4. Experiment with dialogues, e.g. ask one member to act out a discussion between the part of him that likes going to church and the part that is bored by it.

5. If possible, get someone to read up an account of a Perl's 'Dream Seminar' (in *Gestalt Therapy Now*) and let him help another member to explore a recent dream.

7 Yoga

The reports of Institutes of Further Education are not often considered in analyses of social change or economic conditions. The traditional classes such as typing and dressmaking continue. Greater travel has created demands for French cooking, rather than just cooking in general. The price of car servicing has sent people to car maintenance classes. But how do we explain the sharp increase in yoga classes? Earlier I mentioned the stated aim of participants is a desire to learn how to relax. This is not all yoga has to offer and people are attracted by the meditational side about which they have heard a little.

To learn about yoga the best thing is to join a class, but what we can do here is to indicate some of the main features of yoga and see the way in which it can serve the Christian seeking wholeness. Three features seem important to describe. 1. Yoga as a means to help the senses achieve balance. 2. Yoga as a way of increasing 'attention'. 3. Yoga as a way to enter into silence.

The Christian can look at his own and the world's disorder and see it as the consequence of sin entering the world to destroy the perfection of God's original creation or he can see it as an incomplete stage as God works out his purpose of bringing all to final

perfection. Whichever picture he holds in his mind—
both have biblical roots—it describes the idea that
God wills man to seek perfection—a restoration of
the proper original, or final, balance that makes man
fully human. The techniques of yoga can be used to
assist this process. When the body is relaxed and its
different parts rest in balance, when rhythmic breathing allows the person to give attention to his inner life,
when in silence the person opens himself towards
God, then God can come in grace. He can come in
many other ways and when people are using all
manner of techniques, but a lot of experience is
accumulating to say that he does come in this way.

We begin to create a still world in which God's
presence may be more easily recognized by taking up
postures (*asanas*) that require deliberation to achieve
them. We have to put away from our attention many
other things in order to concentrate upon achieving
the posture. We have thus started on a process of
simplification. Instead of our attention being on many
things it is now on one thing. But this concentration
is not fierce. We do not say to ourselves: At all costs
I shall get into that posture. For months I had been
unable to get into 'The Plough'—a posture in which
the body is supported on the shoulders with the legs
stretched over the head and touching the floor. I
wanted to get into this posture and was somewhat
annoyed that I could not when others could. Gradually I became less annoyed by my failure and then it
happened: my toes were touching the floor. When I

55

became released from competition with others, when I was no longer battling with myself, then the posture came. Having achieved a posture smoothly and without haste, one yields to it and relaxes in it. The body becomes still. A first step has been taken towards harmony.

Many manuals are available that describe and ilustrate asanas. We can mention just a few. *The Half-Lotus*: Sit on the floor with both legs bent and feet pointing to the right. Bring the left heel into the groin with the sole flat against the right thigh and the knees on the floor. Hold yourself upright with the arms stretched out and the hands resting on the knees. Gradually it becomes easier to relax into this posture and hold it for considerable periods. *The Tree*: Stand upright with feet together. Bend the right leg and put the right foot against the left thigh close to the groin. Now stretch the arms above the head with palms together. It is easier to keep the balance by looking at and concentrating upon some object level with the eyes. *The Shoulder Stand*: Lie on your back. Bend the knees, then push the legs up vertically, at the same time raising the buttocks and trunk off the floor. Support the trunk by bending the arms and placing the hands in the small of the back. The body should be at right angles to the floor resting on the shoulders. *The Cobra*: Lie face down with the hands flat by the shoulders. Push up until the arms are stretched and the head and chest forms an arc with the lower part of the body from the waist to feet touching the floor.

Correct breathing makes it easier to achieve these postures. In general follow the guide: breathe in before taking the posture; breathe out as you go into the posture; breathe normally as you hold the posture.

The postures of yoga assist the senses to achieve balance. The control of breathing, or pranayana, is a further stage in the process of achieving 'attention' —that is, a focusing upon one's inner life. It has long been known that there is a close connection between breathing and states of mind. 'It took my breath away' is a good descriptive phrase. It is used to describe in physiological terms a feeling. How we feel affects our breathing. Does it work the other way round? By controlling the breathing can we affect our state of mind? The answer is yes. By steadying the rhythm of our breathing we can bring inner calm. As we give attention to our breathing we become more aware of what is going on within us and we find ourselves moving beyond an awareness of how our lungs are functioning to what we are feeling 'internally'. Another element in breathing exercises is more fully to use the potential of our lungs. Most of the time our breathing is shallow. We do not discover this until deliberately we set out to fill our lungs fully by expanding not just the chest as we breathe in but also the abdomen and upper part of the trunk.

Again work with a group or using a manual will permit this aspect of yoga to be more fully explored. For our purpose here some simple exercises can be tried. The simplest of all is to sit comfortably in a relaxed posture and give attention to one's breathing —just noticing it. It is then possible to bring a particular rhythm into it—say the 1.4.2. rhythm in which you inhale to the count of one, hold the breath for a count of four and exhale for a count of two. A further rhythm can be achieved by breathing through alternative nostrils—for example, breathe in through the left nostril (blocking the right nostril with a finger), hold and then out through the right (blocking the left), pause before inhaling through the right and out through the left and so on. However odd all this may sound it does bring calm, taking away anxiety and distraction, and enabling one to focus attention steadily, calmly and effortlessly within oneself.

The aim of yoga is spiritual. It is not an ancient discipline directed to health and beauty. All exercises in posture and breathing are directed towards meditation—what I have called the entry into silence. The Christian using the techniques should do so in order that God's grace may come to him—through meditation prepared for by the exercises. We aim to discover a little of what God is and allow ourselves, as it were, to be washed by that knowledge. After the asanas and pranayama we are sitting, relaxed and calm. We now choose to direct our attention towards God. We shut our eyes and concentrate our attention. The possibilities beyond this point are very wide, but I shall mention here the use of a *mantra*—that is, a word or phrase rich in associations with faith. So, for example, take the early credal sentence 'Jesus is Lord'. Repeat that sentence as you breathe in. Gradually the words become glowing and we feel caught up in the excitement of worship. If the mind begins to wander we gently bring our attention back by means of the mantra. Nothing needs to be forced. The classic Jesus Prayer—'Lord Jesus Christ, Son of God, have mercy on me a sinner'—has been used as a mantra from very early days. Some recommend the use of the 'I am . . .' phrases in the Gospels. Thus as we say, 'I am the Light of the World' our meditation centres upon light. We will not just be thinking about light but pondering it. We turn the object of our meditation around in our imagination like a diamond in our hands. Not only do we then perceive fresh things but we become caught up in what we already know. The truth becomes not an object—a possession. We become possessed by the truth.

As I have suggested, this is but the beginning. The silence prepared for by the exercises of yoga can be used for meditation in any of the traditional ways. One can picture some biblical story or incident and allow it to generate its own life so that one can step into the scene and belong to it. Some picture or symbol can serve as a focus. A whole new world opens up as we find a way to enter into silence.

Books
J.-M. Déchanet, *Christian Yoga* (Search Press, 1964).

H. and F. Wells, *Yoga for all* (BBC Publications, 1973).

Group work

1. Try the postures described.

2. Practice the breathing exercises.

3. Meditate using a mantra or some other image on which to concentrate.

8 Sexuality

Of all human experiences sexual experience is the one where there is the greatest potential for realizing the harmony of body, mind and spirit. Yet the achievement of integration in this area seems so difficult. In sexual experience we can catch a glimpse of harmony, but we never wholly possess it. In this way it serves to remind us of the nature of true health and also the extent of the sickness that perverts even our best expressions of love.

Sexuality is laden with a great deal of disharmony from the traditions we have received concerning it. The ambivalence of the Christian tradition with regard to sex is notorious. We all inherit something of this tradition. We also live at a time when ours is not such a liberated age as some suppose. The excesses of sexual liberation are a rather shrill adolescent rebellion against an inheritance from which the rebels are not themselves free. The chances are that few of us are at ease as far as sexuality is concerned. Groups can experiment by discussing a sexual topic and then exploring together their feelings of anxiety, shame, curiosity and so on. At the level of the intellect it would not be difficult to convince people that sex is good rather than evil—that a world without sexuality would be worse than a world including it.

But clearly we are not governed by our intellects because the majority of people do not regard sex in this way. They find they have feelings that do not cohere with their ideas or ideals.

Sexuality is morally neutral—that is, it is capable of both good and bad use; hence our anxiety. We are not sure that we can use it in a good way. The problem of harmonizing our physicality and our feelings, minds and the strange messages from our intuitive level, is so great that our confidence is shaken. At the moment the odds are stacked against being confident as far as sexuality is concerned. A great deal of literature—books and magazines—is easily available commending a style of sexual activity that has been influenced very greatly by the Masters and Johnson research on human sexual responses at the Reproductive Biology Research Foundation in St Louis. This research, and the attitudes that have grown from it, has been given inadequate criticism. It is not at all clear that, in particular, the human female orgasm described by Masters and Johnson, with their emphasis on the clitoris as the centre of sexual feeling and a certain likeness between the male and female climaxes, is as normal as they suppose. But an orthodoxy in sexology has developed of a somewhat fundamentalist type. It supposes that if sexual experience is not of the approved form then the couple involved are lacking. In this way the literature puts considerable pressure upon normal people, enjoying what are for them normal sexual relations, who are made to feel inadequate because they are different. This is a wicked thing—just as wicked as the repressive attitude the new orthodoxy is concerned to replace. What has gone wrong is that a single aspect of sexuality has been separated from the rest of the experience—in this case a particular physical phenomenon, the clitoral orgasm, that can be achieved by certain techniques of physical stimulation.

It is very obvious that no sexual experience is possible without the physical. Sexuality is so important because it does so firmly recall us to the fact that human life is set within a material world. There is an echo of incarnation about it. But no mature experience of sexuality can be achieved without the physical being integrated with thought, feeling and aspiration. Certain things are important in gaining this integration.

I have been critical of the new sexology because it has got away with too little criticism of the right kind and needs to learn reticence—a quality natural instinct seems to recognize as important in this matter, but to which sexual reformers very often seem blind. I would also want to say that the information about our bodies that is now readily available is not unimportant. It is possible to know it all and be a hopeless lover. Not to know it may not help either. The title of Reuben's book *Everything You Always Wanted to Know About Sex—But Were Afraid to Ask* makes an important point. Some anxiety towards sex is because we have inadequate knowledge. This need not be the case any longer, so long as we do not take all we read as indisputable fact. We can learn what we want to know. We do not need to know all there is to be known, but can know sufficient to save us from the anxiety of ignorance.

It is also possible to learn about available techniques. Here it is important to stress that there are no *right* techniques in sexual relations. There are simply techniques that can be used if a couple choose to use them, just as there are different coital positions to be chosen according to the mood and needs of the couple. Knowledge of techniques and coital positions can be known and then allowed to pass into the back of the mind. Augustine said about orators: 'I think that there is hardly a single eloquent man who can both speak well and think of the rules of eloquence while he is speaking.' I do not think there is a lover who can love well and think of sexual technique at the same time. This is not to say that thought does not play an important part in sexual experience; it does and should, as a partner with other elements, and not in a dominant role.

The interplay of emotions is another element in the experience. How does one communicate emotionally with another person? Words, though not finally adequate, are not to be despised. There can be a communication of silence spoilt by words, but often affective communication is assisted by them. Learning to speak with each other about our feelings is a difficult but important task. Here again we recognize the frailty of one element on its own and the need for a combination of many elements. Love without words is not adequate, nor is a love that depends on words. We need non-verbal forms of communication for any rich human interchange. In sexual experience the range of possible forms of non-verbal communication is greatly extended. But this is not to say that those who lack the opportunity of sexual experience must therefore live at a poor level. Very many spinsters and bachelors prove that this need not be the case. We all miss certain experiences in different ways. The single person may lose the potential enrichment of sexual experience but gain in ways not readily available to the married.

Two of the early Christian Fathers, John Chrysostom and Augustine, spoke of their anxiety about sexual relations because within them there is a 'clouding of reason'—there is a point where one loses self-control. A desire to retain complete control of oneself is not an unusual need in people, and such people may find difficulties in their sexual relations without being able to understand the reason. There may be something of this need in a high proportion of people. Their somewhat obsessive need to be in control makes sexual relations difficult and yet it may be through their sexuality that they will come to health. As they release control—allowing their bodies to respond, their minds to be free and their feelings open—the level of the intuitive, so often crowded out by other elements, comes into its own and a deep quality of human experience and communication with another is achieved. In this way we may have a glimpse of heaven in a much more real way than is meant when the word is used in sentimental songs.

Books
Irving Singer, *The Goals of Human Sexuality* (Wildwood House, 1973).

Group work
1. Share what embarrassments you have in talking about sex.

2. Discuss the attitudes to sex you find held by different people you come across. Bring together magazine articles, agony columns, books and consider the sexual attitudes conveyed by them.

3. How much does curiosity feature in your attitude to sexuality?

9 Worship

Sometimes in worship I find myself reflecting on the oddness of what we are doing. The proverbial Martian, unless he has similar experiences himself, would find it difficult to work out what was happening. He might find some resemblance between worship and game-playing, but would probably discern that the latter was for the enjoyment of the participants but could well be puzzled by the apparent lack of enjoyment of the participants in the former. He could conclude that worship is performed for the benefit of someone other than those taking part. He would be right. Nevertheless I still believe that, though worship is not primarily for our benefit, it should have as a by-product that which is instrumental for our salvation. Worship should direct us towards the goal of human life and serve to bring people nearer to that goal. Worship serves to stimulate various aspects of being human, bind them together and direct them towards the service of God. Worship is a model of the process of salvation we have been describing so far. At least this is an ideal for worship that we ought to be seeking.

Our actual experience is probably very far from this ideal. Worship should in a balanced way utilize and stimulate different parts of us—body, mind and spirit. But we live within traditions in which severe distortions of the ideal have taken place. Protestant worship has been dominated by words—the vehicles of ideas. Why have Protestant churches never claimed the allegiance of the masses? It is because Protestant worship has been centred very largely on that which interests the mass of men least: the intellect. Where Protestant sects have held the attention of those from a working-class culture it is because other elements have been added—as, for example, in the Salvation Army or the Pentecostal churches. Generally the tone has been directive and masculine and there has been only a minor role for succour and the feminine. On the other hand, Catholic worship has traditionally been more feminine in tone; more theatrical and less intellectual. In the Catholic Church there has existed a massive intellectual inheritance, but this has been so powerful that it could almost be taken for granted and certainly not allowed to dominate worship. Less solidly based traditions such as worship of the Sacred Heart or reverence for Mary have been used as vehicles to carry emotional responses to God in worship. In Orthodox worship we have an interesting mixture of elements. What is heard is important: the voice of the priest hidden behind the iconostasis is like the voice of God speaking to his people on earth. What is seen is not undervalued: there is the extreme theatricality of the Great and Little Entrances when the bread and wine for the eucharist and the gospel books are processed through the church into the sanctuary. There are the icons which are both seen and touched. But the dominant feature is the sense of community that binds the congregation together in spite of the fact that they have no overt part in the liturgy. It is clear that the weight worship has to carry is intolerable. It may have the responsibility for setting out the whole process of redemption, but it is shaped by the unredeemed and inevitably bears within itself the distortions of the all-too-human within the Body of Christ.

What we can do, and must do, is to attempt to enrich the tradition we have inherited with elements that do not displace the previously dominant characteristics but complement them. Thus if the dominant tone has been intellectual an attempt must be made to add to this emotional elements. Similarly if the tone has been primarily emotional an injection of intellectual qualities will be important. The practical danger of attempting this is that the added elements can either in reality or imagination seem to displace rather than complement the existing features. I find that one characteristic of human nature I have to learn to tolerate with good humour is the readiness to assume that if one thing is being commended something else is being condemned. For example, if you are commending sacramental worship you must be devaluing preaching. This is very silly but human, and we have to continue our attempts at better balances of different features with good courage.

Much has been written in recent years about the

possibilities for adding to our inherited traditions of worship. Less, I think, about the purpose of this experimentation. We can here mention a few things to serve as stimulants to the discussion of this large subject. If our bodies must be part of the harmony of the whole person they should figure in worship. Of course they do in that we, in our bodies, are present in the congregation. I would like to see physicality have a more manifest role in worship. We would do well to avoid extremes for the reason I have stated earlier. It is all too easy to spoil creative endeavours by alienating those involved through moving too quickly beyond the latitude of innovation they are prepared to accept. I do not commend nudity in worship. I do think we could touch each other more. The kiss of peace has broken the ice for many people. There is a danger of sticking at this point with a highly stylized token of body-contact that defeats its primary purpose. I find it somewhat comic to see married couples shaking hands in church and children used to being hugged by their parents solemnly shaking their hands. A kiss or hug in church might be a powerful declaration that any touching is not necessarily a first step towards sexual intercourse or homosexuality. Harvey Cox suggested that some form of massage might be the next step in liturgical reform. As I have indicated I am not against massage, but in worship all I ask for is honest and warm human contact.

The use of bodies in their expressive capacity in

dance has much to commend it. As someone has said, dance can be a praying with the bones. For some the sight of dancing may help, while for others it will be important to be a participant—to feel in the limbs what they want to say about God and to God. Music has been the traditional way in which emotion has been able to be expressed in worship. Colour in a static form through stained glass can have the effect of giving a general tone to the worship space. I have been involved in effective experiments in which emotional tone is modified by coloured lights. The smell of flowers or incense can also function in this area. The opportunities for development are limited only by the imagination.

Most important of all for the expression of, and means to, the goal of integration are the sacraments. As salvation came to the world in 'the Word made flesh' so it is both declared and mediated in acts that also have the form of incarnation. Christ, becoming in some way united with the physical world in bread and wine, enters our bodies in order to bring salvation to our whole person—body, mind and spirit. That which is the basis of our redemption becomes both symbol and instrument of it. No language is adequate to describe God, and man has to use words in a special way in order to talk about him. He must use analogies with the world we know but press them to breaking point. He must use the language of the myth—the story that can be read in two ways—at one level it seems to belong wholly to the world we know, but at a second it is pointing us towards the mystery of God. The language of faith is of an incarnational type. It uses ordinary words in such a way as to evoke the extraordinary. So in sacramental worship things of our earth are used in their ordinariness for an extraordinary purpose—that of recalling God to further, in an incarnational form, the redemption he began in such a form in Christ. In this way we are pointed to a redemption that seeks the integration of the whole person—body, mind and spirit.

Books
C. Vagaggini, *The Flesh, Instrument of Salvation* (Alpha House, New York, 1969).
ed. J. G. Davies, *Worship and Dance* (University of Birmingham, 1975).
Harvey Cox, *The Seduction of the Spirit* (Wildwood House, 1974).
J. Killinger, *Leave it to the Spirit* (SCM Press, 1971).

Group work
1. Does worship make any sense against the background of the attitudes we have been discussing so far?

2. If it is true that an ideal of worship has been distorted in different traditions, where do you recognize the distortions in the traditions you know?

3. Think out how a ceremony of feet-washing could be incorporated into an act of worship.

WORSHIP

4. Share your experiences of different experiments in worship.

5. What does the Lord's Supper mean to you? Does it make connections with different parts of your life and help to integrate them?

10 Wholeness in Community

In this final chapter what we must do is attempt to correct an imbalance in what we have considered so far. Most of our attention has been focused on the individual and the dynamics of the relationships, as it were, within him. Some notice has been taken of the person in his relationships with others, but the impression could have been made that if we can achieve internal harmony then we have gained health. This is far from being true.

We cannot understand human beings on their own, but only in their relationships. A corpuscular model for the person is inadequate. The person is defined by a complex system composed of interlocking and interacting sub-systems. The moment we try to visualize what this means it is apparent that we are dealing with something too complex to be integrated by a single image. Man is what he is within himself; what goes on in his family relationships; what happens in his various social groupings; what he is at work; what happens to him as a result of the political framework within which he lives. These sub-systems combine to form the complex system of the person. In general terms we can say that what happens in one sub-system affects the whole. What we do not know is precisely how this happens and to what degree—

although we are beginning to know a great deal about it. Different people seem to put different filters between one sub-system and another. For example, if a man has a quarrel at work what effect will that have on his relationship with his wife? In one case the man will take out on his wife his anger against his work-mate. In another case the man blocks out the connections between the work and family sub-systems and there is little effect. The whole matter is so complex that we should be somewhat reticent about making sweeping claims about the power of the Gospel to renovate the whole life of man. We may be convinced that this is the case, but we do well not to claim it in a glib fashion. The work of redemption has to be as complex as man is.

Everyone in education and the helping professions knows that whatever influence they have on others will be mostly undone by a sort of self-correcting mechanism that comes into action the moment a change is begun. Some marvellous work was done at a psychiatric clinic where I was chaplain. People were taken out of their setting and helped to understand themselves and their problems more fully. It was exciting to see change taking place. Then they returned to their homes or work and the old pressures were re-exerted and a lot of ground was lost. Similarly teachers may quicken in a pupil an interest in, say, literature knowing that the values of the group to which he belongs will be against its being maintained. There seems a little evidence that more permanent change is more likely when intervention is made into two or more sub-systems at the same time. This is why looking at new ideas in a group context can be so important. The idea affects internal and social relationships at the same time.

The way in which the individual is locked into a system is clearly seen in the family. In a healthy family he will be free to be himself and he will be able to exert an influence upon the other members so that the whole system can change its direction. One part interacts with and affects the others. In a disturbed family members tend to control the contributions of others so that the stability of the system is not endangered. Power in the family will probably be held by a single dominating member. Individuals will not be clearly distinguished from the whole unit so that one member can speak for the others. In these and other ways the family will be kept in a somewhat apathetic equilibrium. The pressure exerted by such a system on an individual member is very great indeed. If we look at much larger systems similar criteria of health and disturbance can be applied. Most democrats would like to think that they lived in a healthy society. Honesty would compel us to recognize marks of considerable disturbance in the body politic. Society conspires to act sometimes in a disturbed way; sometimes in a healthy way. Between the disturbed and healthy family one can see a number of in-between stages. One characteristic of some families in this area is the way in which they select a member to take responsibilty for the evil of the group as a whole. Such a scapegoating procedure applies also in society at large. Special groups are selected to carry the burden of the failure of society. In particular the poor serve this role. This is the kernel of the Marxist doctrine of poverty. The poor are not so because of their innate limitations. Their poverty is externally imposed on them by an exploiting society. On the basis of this analysis the Marxist sees no hope in alleviation, but only in a revolution that will change the power structure of society in such a way as to make exploitation no longer possible.

If the Gospel is concerned with making whole the total person then the Church must be concerned to influence change in the political and other structures that affect the health of people. This can be done in many ways. The Church should give much more attention to how it can affect the morale of the community. If people feel more secure and are together motivated by a sense of purpose, then morale improves and with it the whole health of the community. It has been suggested that if there was a fall of 5 per cent in loving acts towards elderly people in a city the size of Sheffield, 50,000 places in hospitals or old people's homes would be required to replace them.

The Church can earn its living in society, but this will be a by-product of its concern for total health. Another area in which influence can be exerted is in what is loosely called community work. In the past the Church has been somewhat patronizing in its community work—as were most other social institutions. It has tended to do things for people. Such a style of work has become increasingly offensive to people. It is also counterproductive of the values we seek to support. If we do things for people we keep them as children and do not assist their growth—we take away human dignity rather than confer it. An alternative style of working is usually called Community Development. Here we try to help the community to locate and respond to its own needs together. It keeps the responsibility for changing things in the community with the people who are the community. In this way it brings more human resources to bear upon the problems of the community; it prevents the political authorities becoming the scapegoats for the failure of society; it maintains human dignity. The Church must also be seeking to create an involvement with the wider political life of society. There are some things that will never be put right in the nation until the law is changed. A small but significant example would be the brutalization of man by blood sports. There are many others. Changes in the ordering of society do not just happen, they occur because someone somewhere takes action.

However successfully we learn to relax, to repossess our bodies and emotions, to learn to meditate and so on, it will be an irresponsible luxury and self-indulgence unless we pay attention to the social dimension of health.

Books

R. A. Lambourne, *Community, Church and Healing* (Darton, Longman and Todd, 1963).

F. Milson, *Community Work and the Christian Faith* (Hodder and Stoughton, 1975).

Group work

1. Does this 'systems' view of the person make sense? Share examples of the ways in which one part of life affects another.

2. Are the poor inadequate or exploited?

3. Is the morale of a community very important? How can it be improved?

4. Ask a member to explore the principles of Community Development further and then discuss them with the group.

5. 'All that is needed for evil to succeed is that good men do nothing.' Is this true? If so how do you react to it? Does it mean that the Church must be involved in politics? Why do you think many Christians are scared of this?